Sugar Fre
Cookbook

Healthy And Delicious Sugar Free Diet Dessert Recipes For Losing Weight

Table of Contents

Introduction

Plenty of research has shown that reducing sugar in your diet is key for losing weight, lowering your risk for cancer and reducing inflammation among many other health benefits. With all these wonderful benefits that reducing sugar has on your health, you may wonder why most people do not cut sugar out of their diet. There is a easy yet troubling explanation for this problem, and it is that sugar is very addictive.

Like quitting smoking, eliminating your sugar cravings can be extremely difficult. This baking cookbook is designed to help you beat your sugar cravings, by giving you delicious sugar free cake, cookie and pie recipes. These recipes will make you forget that you are on a sugar free diet!

Good luck, we hope you enjoy these sugar free baking and dessert recipes.

Chapter 1: Sugar Free Cake And Square Recipes

Cinnamon Coffee Cake

Ingredients

3 1/2 ounces almond flour, 1 cup

4 ounces cream cheese, softened

1/3 cup granular Splenda, not liquid

1 teaspoon cinnamon

1/4 cup cold butter, diced

1/2 teaspoon baking powder

1/4 teaspoon baking soda

1/3 cup sour cream

1 egg

1 teaspoon vanilla

1 egg

2 tablespoons granular Splenda

1/8 teaspoon vanilla

1/8 teaspoon cinnamon

Directions

In a medium bowl, mix the almond flour, 1/3 cup Splenda and cinnamon. Cut in the butter with a pastry cutter until coarse crumbs form. Set aside 1/2 cup of the crumb mixture for the topping and keep chilled until needed.

To the remaining crumb mixture, add the baking powder, baking soda, sour cream, 1 egg and 1 teaspoon vanilla. Beat on medium speed until well blended. The batter will be thin. Spread in a greased 8" round cake pan.

In the same bowl, beat the cream cheese, 1 egg, 2 tablespoons Splenda, 1/8 teaspoon vanilla and 1/8 teaspoon cinnamon until smooth. The filling will be thin. Spoon over the batter. Top with the reserved crumb mixture. Bake at 350F 30-35 minutes or until golden brown.

Nutrition: 293 calories; 27 g fat; 7 g carbohydrates; 8 g protein; per 1/6 of recipe

Pumpkin Pecan Cheesecake Bars

Ingredients

2 cups whole pecans

1 tsp cinnamon

1 tbsp coconut oil

10-15 drops liquid stevia

1 pinch sea salt

Filling

8 oz. cream cheese

1/4 cup heavy cream

10 oz. pumpkin puree

2 tsp vanilla extract

20 drops liquid stevia

1/2 cup powdered erythritol

1/4 tsp pumpkin pie spice

1 tsp cinnamon

1 pinch salt

2 large eggs

Frosting

2 oz. cream cheese

2 tbsp heavy cream

1/4 cup powdered erythritol

1/2 tsp vanilla extract

Directions

Preheat the oven to 350°F. Combine all the crust ingredients in a food processor and pulse until the pecans are a fine crumb texture.

Line a 9x6-inch baking dish with parchment paper, letting two sides spill over for easy removal. Press the crust into the dish, making one even layer. Bake for 12 minutes, then let cool.

Use an electric hand mixer and beat the cream cheese and heavy cream until fully combined and even throughout. Then, add in the pumpkin puree, vanilla extract and liquid stevia and combine.

Add in the erythritol, pumpkin pie spice, cinnamon and a pinch of salt and combine. Add in one egg at a time, incorporating each before adding another.

Once the crust has cooled a bit, pour the pumpkin cheesecake batter into the baking dish. Reduce the heat in the oven to 325°F and bake for 25-30 minutes. Refrigerate for 6 hours.

To make the frosting, combine all the frosting ingredients and beat with an electric hand mixer until light and fluffy. Frost the top of the cheesecake bars.

Pecan Chocolate Cake

Ingredients

4 ounces unsweetened baking chocolate, broken up

1/3 cup water

1/3 cup vegetable oil

3/4 cup pecans, toasted and cooled

1/4 cup unsweetened cocoa powder

1/4 cup soya powder

12 large eggs, room temperature, separated

2 1/4 cups granular sugar substitute, divided

2 teaspoons powdered ginger

1/4 teaspoon cream of tarter

Vegetable oil spray for greasing pan

Directions

Preheat oven to 325F. Grease the bottom of a 10-inch tube pan, and line with parchment or waxed paper. Place chocolate and the water in a microwavable bowl; microwave on high 1 to 2 minutes, until chocolate is melted, checking at 1-minute intervals.

Stir until smooth, cool to lukewarm, then stir in oil; set aside.In a food processor, pulse pecans, cocoa powder and bake mix until pecans are finely ground. In a large bowl, beat egg yolks with cup sugar substitute on high speed with an electric mixer, until light and fluffy, about 5 minutes.

Stir in melted chocolate, pecan mixture and ginger. In another large bowl, beat egg whites and cream of tartar on medium-high speed with an electric mixer, until frothy.

Gradually add remaining sugar substitute, beating until stiff peaks form. With a rubber spatula, fold one-third of the meringue into the yolk mixture to lighten; fold in the remaining meringue until just combined.

Pour batter evenly in prepared pan and bake until a toothpick inserted in center of cake comes out clean, about 45 minutes. Allow cake to cool for 30 minutes before removing from pan. To remove: Run a knife around the inner and outer rim of cake, place a wire rack or plate over pan, and invert.

Remove pan, and peel off paper. Cool completely before cutting

Lemon Cake

Ingredients

1 (16-ounce) package sugar-free yellow cake mix

2 (4-serving-size) packages instant sugar-free, fat-free lemon pudding and pie filling

1 cup fat-free evaporated milk

1/2 cup canola oil

1/2 cup water

2 teaspoons lemon extract, divided

1 cup egg substitute

1 (8-ounce) container frozen sugar-free whipped topping, thawed

3 to 4 drops yellow food coloring

Directions

Preheat oven to 350 F. Coat a Bundt pan with cooking spray.

In a large bowl, beat cake mix, pudding mix, evaporated milk, oil, water, and 1 teaspoon lemon extract until smooth. Beat in egg substitute until well combined, then pour into Bundt pan.

Bake 40 to 45 minutes, or until a wooden toothpick inserted in center comes out clean. Cool 15 minutes, then remove from pan to cool completely.

In a medium bowl, combine whipped topping, yellow food coloring, and remaining lemon extract; mix until thoroughly combined. Spread evenly over cake.

Serve immediately, or refrigerate until ready to serve.

Moist Chocolate Cake

Ingredients

1/3 cup water

1/4 teaspoon salt

9 oz coconut oil

3 oz cocoa powder

2/3 cup butter

4 large eggs

1/2 cup Erythritol

1/2 cup sucralose artificial sweetener

Directions

Line bottom of 9-inch springform pan with parchment paper.

In small pot, heat water, salt, and Erythritol and sucralose over medium heat until salt and sweetener are dissolved. Melt coconut oil and mix in cocoa powder.

Mix chocolate and butter in large bowl with electric mixer. Beat in the hot water mixture. The mixture will appear very runny, it will thicken when you add eggs.

Add in egg, one at a time, beating well after adding each. Pour mix into prepared springform pan. Wrap outside well with foil.

Place springform pan in larger cake pan and add boiling water to the outside pan about 1 inch deep. Bake cake in water bath for 45 minutes at 350°F. Remove and cool slightly on wire rack.

Chill cake in refrigerator, then remove side of springform pan. Cut into 12 pieces and serve with whipped cream.

Sugar Free Brownies

Ingredients

6 tablespoons butter

1/3 cup erythritol

1/3 cup cocoa powder

1 egg

1/2 tsp vanilla extract

1 pinch salt

1/4 cup almond flour

1/2 teaspoon baking powder

1/4 cup walnuts

1 tablespoon natural peanut butter

1 tablespoon butter

Directions

Preheat your oven to 350F.

Melt your butter on a small pan and let erythritol, or your choice of granulated sweetener dissolve it in.

Pour the butter and erythritol into a mixing bowl and add your cocoa powder, salt and vanilla extract. Add in an egg and beat until thoroughly combined.

Add almond flour and baking powder to help the brownie rise a bit. Pour your brownie batter into a 6 inch cast iron skillet.

Place the skillet brownie into the oven and bake for about 30 minutes. The top will be set but slightly soft. Do not over-bake, the brownie will continue cooking after being removed from oven.

Banana Peanut Butter Cake

Ingredients

3/4 cup all-purpose flour

1/2 teaspoon baking powder

1/2 teaspoon baking soda

1/4 teaspoon salt

1/4 cup margarine, light, softened

1/3 cup Stevia

1 egg

1/4 cup natural peanut butter

2 tablespoons reduced-fat sour cream

1 large ripe banana, mashed

Directions

Preheat the oven to 350 F. Coat an 8-inch round cake pan with cooking spray.

In a small bowl, combine the flour, baking powder, baking soda, and salt; mix well and set aside.

In a large bowl, cream the butter and Stevia. Add the egg, peanut butter, sour cream, and banana; mix well.

Add the flour mixture; mix well, then spread into the cake pan.

Bake for 30 to 35 minutes, or until a wooden toothpick inserted in the center comes out clean. Let cool in the pan for 10 minutes, then remove from the pan to cool completely before cutting into wedges.

Almond Spice Cake

Ingredients

1 cup milk

1 tbsp white vinegar

2 tbsp butter - softened

2 tbsp shortening - softened

3/4 cup Splenda granulated

1/2 tsp vanilla

1 large egg

1/2 tsp ground cinnamon

1/8 tsp ground cloves

1/8 tsp ground ginger

1/8 tsp ground allspice

1/2 tsp baking powder

1/2 tsp baking soda

1 cup almond flour

Directions

Preheat oven to 350 degrees. Prepare 8" square baking dish by either spraying with Baker's Joy or grease the sides. Mix vinegar and milk. Set aside.

In medium mixing bowl, cream together butter and shortening. Blend in Splenda. Add vanilla and egg. Mix until well blended.

Add spices, baking powder, and baking soda. Stir to mix. Begin adding almond flour and milk mixture alternately, stirring until just mixed after each addition.

Pour into baking dish. Bake for 40 minutes at 350F. Allow to cool on a wire rack for 1 hour. Cake will be extremely moist and very dense.

Chocolate Cheesecake

Ingredients

1 cup almond flour

4 tbsp butter

1 tbsp cocoa powder

1/2 tsp cinnamon

1/16 tsp Stevia

1 pinch salt

Filling

16 oz cream cheese softened

3/4 cup erythritol

2 eggs

1/2 cup sour cream

3 oz unsweetened baker's chocolate

1 tbsp cocoa powder

1 pinch salt

1 tsp vanilla extract

Directions

Preheat oven to 350°F. To make the crust. melt 4 tbsp of butter and combine with almond flour, cocoa powder, cinnamon and Stevia. Mix well.

Press the crust dough into a 9-inch springform pan and bake in the oven for about 15 minutes or until the crust is solid and darker.

While the crust is baking, begin making your cheesecake filling! Beat cream cheese and erythritol with an electric hand mixer until smooth. Add in sour cream, vanilla extract, salt and 2 eggs and beat with the mixer until creamy.

Melt 3 oz. of unsweetened baker's chocolate in a double boiler or just in a small pan, on low heat, stirring constantly.

Pour the chocolate and 1 tbsp of cocoa powder into your cream cheese mixture. Stir with a spoon/rubber spatula to combine the chocolate and cream cheese mixture.

Now pour your cheesecake batter into the springform pan on top of your crisp almond flour crust. Bake in the oven for 50-60 minutes or until the top of the cheesecake is set and darker.

Let the cheesecake cool to room temperature and then refrigerate overnight or atleast 4 hours.

When the cake has chilled, run a plastic knife along the edges of the springform pan to loosen any cake that has stuck to the pan.

Undo the buckle and remove the pan's edges. Slice and serve with whipped cream and a square of dark chocolate if desired

Frosted Orange Cake

Ingredients

1 orange cut into quarters

6 eggs

2 1/2 cups almond flour

1 tsp baking powder

4 tbsp granulated Splenda

1 tsp vanilla

1/4 tsp salt

Icing

1/2 cup natural yogurt unsweetened

4 oz cream cheese softened

1.8 oz powdered sweetener

2 tbsp orange zest

Directions

Place the orange quarters in the food processor and using the blade attachment, remove all seed before processing. Process until pureed.

Add all the other ingredients. Pulse until smooth. Pour into two greased and lined sponge pans.

Bake at 350F for 20-25 minutes. Test the centre with a skewer to check for doneness.

To Make Icing

Mix the softened cream cheese with the natural yoghurt with a fork until smooth.

Add the orange zest and powdered sweetener.

When the cakes are completely cold, place the first layer on the serving plate and ice with the icing mix. Place the other cake layer on top and sprinkle with the icing mixture and small pieces of orange zest and orange slices.

Lemon Pound Cake

Ingredients

9 lemons

2 3/4 cups all-purpose flour

3/4 cup Splenda Sugar Blend

1 1/2 teaspoons baking powder

3/4 cup heavy cream

6 large eggs

11 tablespoons unsalted butter, melted

1 1/2 cups water

Raspberry Topping:

1 cup Splenda Sugar Blend

1/4 cup water

2 tablespoons Splenda Sugar Blend

2 cups fresh or frozen raspberries

Directions

Preheat oven to 350°F. Grease a 9-by-5-inch loaf pan, line with parchment or waxed paper. Grease paper.

Prepare lemon segments. Grate zest of 4 lemons; slice tops and bottoms off 3 (reserve fourth). Stand lemons on end on a cutting board, and cut away white pith until the flesh is exposed. Over a bowl, cut segments from membranes, letting fruit and juice fall into bowl - remove seeds. With fork, break segments into 1-inch pieces.

Sift flour, Splenda Sugar Blend for Baking, and baking powder into the bowl of an electric mixer. Begin mixing on low speed then add cream. Increase speed to medium, and beat in eggs, one at a time, then butter.

Fold lemon segments, juices, and 3 tablespoons zest gently into batter. Scrape into pan. Bake for 45 to 60 minutes.

Make the glaze while the cake is baking. Juice and zest the remaining 6 lemons. Put Splenda Sugar Blend for Baking in a pot, and add 1 1/2 cups water. Bring to a simmer, and cook, stirring, until sugar dissolves. Stir in lemon juice and remaining zest, and let cool.

Place cake pan on a wire rack for 30 minutes when cake is done. Adjust oven temperature to 350°F (175°C).

Unmold cake, and transfer it to a pie pan or deep dish. Pour lemon syrup over cake, and very gently squeeze the cake to help it absorb syrup. Carefully turn cake upside down in syrup, and squeeze a bit more. Put cake on a baking sheet; return to oven for 10 minutes to set the glaze.

Cool on a rack while making topping

For Raspberry Topping: Combine Splenda Sugar Blend for Baking with 1/4 cup water in a small pot and bring to a boil, stirring until sugar dissolves. Cool completely.

Purée raspberries and syrup in a blender, then strain through a fine sieve. Serve cake with raspberry topping.

Coconut Cake

Ingredients

8 eggs

3/4 cup Splenda

1 tablespoon coconut extract

2/3 cup sifted soy flour

1 teaspoon baking powder

1/2 cup unsalted butter, melted and cooled

6 egg whites

3/4 cup sugar substitute (Splenda)

1/4 teaspoon salt

1 1/2 cups unsalted butter, softened

2/3 cup unsweetened shredded coconut

Directions

Heat oven to 350F. Grease two 8-inch cake pans; line bottoms with parchment paper; grease again. With an electric mixer on high, beat eggs, sugar substitute, and extract until ribbons form, about 5 minutes.

Sift bake mix over egg mixture; fold in with a rubber spatula to combine. Fold in butter. Pour batter into prepared pans. Bake 22 minutes until cake bounces back in middle when lightly touched.

Cool in pans on wire racks 5 minutes. Line racks with paper towels and invert cake layers. Gently peel off parchment. Cool completely.

To Make Frosting:

In a double boiler or a bowl placed over simmering water, whisk egg whites, sugar substitute and salt until temperature reaches 130°F. Transfer whites to mixing bowl and beat on high speed until cool.

Reduce speed to medium and beat in butter until well combined. Place one cake layer on serving plate. Mix 1 cup frosting with half the coconut; frost bottom layer. Place top cake layer over bottom layer. Cover top and sides with remaining frosting. Frost cake with remaining coconut frosting.

Walnut Oatmeal Coffee Cake

Ingredients

1/3 cup canola oil

1/2 cup egg substitute

1/4 cup sugar substitute

1/2 cup plus 1 tablespoon brown sugar, divided

1 teaspoon vanilla extract

3/4 cup quick-cooking oatmeal, prepared in water

3/4 cup white whole wheat flour

3/4 cup all-purpose flour

1 teaspoon cinnamon

1/2 teaspoon salt

1 teaspoon baking soda

1/4 cup chopped walnuts

Directions

Preheat oven to 350 degrees F. Coat an 8-inch square baking dish with cooking spray.

In a large bowl, combine oil, egg substitute, sugar substitute, 1/2 cup brown sugar, the vanilla, and oatmeal; mix well.

In a medium bowl, combine both flours, cinnamon, salt, and baking soda; mix well. Stir flour mixture into egg mixture until well combined. Pour into baking dish.

In a small bowl, mix walnuts and remaining brown sugar; sprinkle over batter.

Bake 30 to 35 minutes, or until toothpick inserted in center comes out dry. Let cool, then cut into squares.

New York Cheesecake

Ingredients

32 ounces cream cheese, room temperature

1 cup Erythritol

5 large eggs, room temperature

1/3 cup heavy whipping cream (double cream)

1 tablespoon lemon zest

1 teaspoon pure vanilla extract

Directions

Grease, or spray with Pam, a 9 inch springform pan. Place the springform pan on a larger baking pan to catch any leakage while the cheesecake is baking.

Preheat oven to 350 degrees F with rack in center of oven.

To Make Filling: In bowl of your electric mixer place the cream cheese and sugar. Beat on medium speed until smooth, scraping down the bowl as needed. Add the eggs, one at a time, beating well after each addition. Scrape down the sides of the bowl. Add the whipping cream, lemon zest, vanilla extract and beat until incorporated. Pour the filling in the greased pan and place the cheesecake pan on a larger baking pan and place in the oven.

Bake for 15 minutes and then lower the oven temperature to 250 F and continue to bake for about another 60 minutes or until firm and only the center of the cheesecake looks moist and wobbles.

Remove from oven and carefully run a knife or spatula around the inside edge of pan to loosen the cheesecake

Let cool completely before covering and refrigerate several hours.

Chocolate Pumpkin Squares

Ingredients

1 1/3 cups all-purpose flour

1/4 cup Splenda Brown Sugar Blend

1/2 cup Splenda Sugar Blend - divided use

1 cup old-fashioned oats

1/2 cup chopped walnuts

3/4 cup light margarine

1 (8-ounce) container fat-free cream cheese

3 large eggs

1 (15-ounce) can pumpkin

1 tablespoon pumpkin pie spice

1 cup sugar free mini chocolate chips

Directions

Bake in a preheated oven at 350°F (175°C). Line a 13X9 pan with foil and spray with a non-stick cooking spray. Set aside.

Combine flour, Splenda Brown Sugar Blend, half of the Splenda Sugar Blend, oats and walnuts. Cut in the margarine with a fork until the mixture is crumbly.

Press all but one cup of the crust mixture into the bottom of the prepared pan. Bake for 15 minutes. Allow to cool.

Beat cream cheese, eggs, the remaining half of the Splenda® Sugar Blend, the pumpkin and the pumpkin pie spice until it is well blended. Pour the cream cheese mixture over the pre-baked crust and sprinkle with the 1 cup of remaining crust and the chocolate chips.

Bake for 25 minutes or until set. Lift from pan to cool.

Vanilla Pound Cake

Ingredients

1/2 cup butter, softened

4 ounces cream cheese, softened

1 cup granular Splenda

5 eggs, room temperature

1 teaspoon lemon extract

1 teaspoon vanilla

6 1/2 ounces almond flour, 1 1/2 cups plus 2 tablespoons

1 teaspoon baking powder

Dash of salt

Directions

Cream the butter, cream cheese and Splenda with an electric mixer. Add the eggs, one at a time; blend in the extracts. Mix the almond flour, salt and baking powder; add to the egg mixture a little at a time.

Pour into a well greased 9-inch round cake pan, spring form pan, or bundt pan. Bake at 350F° 50-55 minutes.

Check the cake for doneness after 40 minutes. The cake will be golden brown and firm to the touch when done. Let cool before serving.

Pumpkin Cheese Cake

Ingredients

16 oz cream cheese

6 eggs

1/2 cup sugar free maple syrup

1 cup canned unsweetened pumpkin

3/8 tsp Stevia extract powder

1 tsp cinnamon

1/4 tsp nutmeg

Directions

Preheat oven to 350F. Combine all ingredients in a mixer and blend until smooth.

Pour into a deep dish pie pan that has been sprayed with non stick cooking spray.

Bake for 50 - 55 minutes or until center is set. Remove from oven, let cool then chill completely.

Chocolate Bundt Cake

Ingredients

2 cups almond flour

2 tablespoons coconut flour

1 cup erythritol

1.5 teaspoon baking soda

1/2 teaspoon salt

1 cup butter

1/2 cup cocoa powder

1 cup water

3 large eggs

2 teaspoon vanilla extract

1/2 cup sour cream

Glaze

2 oz. cocoa butter wafers/chips (sugar free white chocolate)

3 tablespoon powdered erythritol

1 teaspoon vanilla extract

2 tablespoon heavy cream

Directions

Preheat your oven to 350°F and start by whisking together 2 cups of blanched almond flour with your coconut flour, erythritol, baking soda and salt.

In a small pot, heat together butter, cocoa powder and water on medium heat. Whisk continuously until combined and then take it off the heat.

Pour in half the chocolate mixture into the dry ingredients and stir to combine. Once its thick to stir, pour in the other half and combine. Add in 1 egg at a time to cake batter. Add sour cream and vanilla extract and stir.

Pour the batter into a greased bundt cake pan and bake for about 40-50 minutes or once a wooden skewer stuck into the middle comes out clean.

While the cake is baking, prepare white chocolate glaze. Melt 2 oz. of organic cocoa butter wafers. Then add powdered erythritol and mix to combine. Add in heavy cream and allow this mixture to chill in the fridge, stirring every 5 minutes.

Once the white chocolate has chilled to the right consistency - thick and opaque in color, pulse it for a few seconds in a blender until smooth.

When bundt cake is finished baking, let it cool in the pan for 10 minutes. Then invert it onto a plate or cooling rack on a baking sheet and let it cool completely.

Once cake is cool to the touch, glaze the cake. Take spoonfuls of your white chocolate glaze and let it drape over the top of the cake and onto the baking sheet.

Sugar Free Marble Cake

Ingredients

3 tablespoons Dutch process cocoa

1 tablespoon Splenda Sugar Blend for Baking

1/4 teaspoon baking soda

2 1/2 tablespoons hot water

2 cups sifted cake flour

1/2 cup Splenda Sugar Blend for Baking

2 1/2 teaspoons baking powder

1/4 teaspoon salt

1/2 cup butter

2 large eggs, lightly beaten

2/3 cup milk

1 teaspoon vanilla extract

Directions

Preheat oven to 325°F (160°C). Grease and flour a 6-cup Bundt pan or an 8x4-inch loaf pan. Set aside.

Combine cocoa, 1 tablespoon Splenda Sugar Blend for Baking, and baking soda; gradually stir in hot water to form a paste. Set aside.

Combine flour, Splenda Sugar Blend for Baking, baking powder, and salt in a large mixing bowl. Cut butter into flour mixture with a fork or a pastry blender until crumbly. This procedure may be done with a mixer at the lowest speed - Cover mixing bowl with a clean tea towel to prevent spattering.

Combine eggs, milk, and vanilla in a small mixing bowl; add 1/3 of the egg mixture to flour mixture. Beat at low speed of an electric mixer until blended. Beat at medium speed for 30 seconds or until batter is smooth, stopping to scrape down sides of bowl. Repeat procedure 2 times.

Set aside half of the batter. Add cocoa mixture to remaining batter, beating at low speed until blended. Alternate light and dark batters by tablespoonfuls into prepared pan. Gently swirl batters with a knife to create a marble effect.

Bake 45 to 50 minutes or until a wooden pick inserted in center comes out clean. Cool in pan on a wire rack 10 minutes. Remove from pan; cool completely on a wire rack.

Apple Spice Cake

Ingredients

Cake:
1 cup all-purpose flour

1 cup whole wheat pastry flour

1 1/2 teaspoons baking powder

1 1/2 teaspoons baking soda

1/2 teaspoon salt

1 1/2 teaspoons ground cinnamon

1/2 teaspoon apple pie spice

1 large egg, lightly beaten

1/2 cup canola oil

3/4 cup Splenda Granulated

1/2 cup 1% low-fat milk

1 tablespoon apple juice or apple cider

1 teaspoon vanilla extract

1 1/2 cups chopped apple

1/2 cup chopped walnuts

Topping:
1 cup whole wheat pastry flour

1/2 cup Splenda Granulated

1 teaspoon ground cinnamon

1/2 teaspoon baking powder

1/4 cup canola oil

1/4 cup chopped walnuts

Directions

Preheat oven to 350°F (175°C). Spray a 9x9x2-inch baking pan with vegetable cooking spray. Set aside.

Combine flours, baking powder, soda, salt, and spices in a large mixing bowl. Set aside.

Combine egg, canola oil, milk, juice, vanilla, and Splenda Granulated in a small mixing bowl. Add liquid mixture to dry ingredients, stirring just until moistened. Stir in apples and walnuts. Spoon mixture into prepared pan.

Combine flour, Splenda Granulated Sweetener, cinnamon, and baking powder. Add oil stirring until blended. Stir in walnuts. Sprinkle topping over the batter.

Bake for 25 minutes or until a wooden pick inserted in center comes out clean.

Chapter 2: Sugar Free Cookie Recipes

Coconut Flour Cookies

Ingredients

1 cup coconut flour sifted

1½ teaspoons Baking Powder

¼ teaspoon pink Himalayan salt

¾ cup Truvia

5 tablespoons coconut oil

½ cup butter

4 large eggs

1 teaspoon vanilla bean paste

1 tablespoon coconut milk

Directions

Stir together coconut flour, baking powder, and salt in a bowl. In a different bowl, whisk butter and coconut oil together.

Add your desired sweetener and whisk until fluffy. Add eggs, almond milk, vanilla bean paste and whisk thoroughly.

Combine dry ingredients with wet ingredients, whisking until thoroughly combined. The dough should have a thick consistency. Add more coconut flour if too thin.

Flatten out with a rolling pin for your desired girth. We are aiming for around ¼ inch. Cut out circular shapes for your cookies.

Place dough onto a silicone mat or an ungreased cookie sheet. Bake at 360°F for 8-10 minutes until edges begin to brown.

Chocolate Peanut Butter Cookies

Ingredients

1 cup creamy peanut butter

1 egg

1/4 cup stevia sweetener

2 tablespoons unsweetened cocoa powder

1 tablespoon vanilla extract

Directions

Preheat oven to 350 degrees F (175 degrees C).

Combine peanut butter, egg, stevia sweetener, cocoa powder, and vanilla extract together with a mixer or food processor. Roll dough into 1-inch balls. Place 1 to 2 inches apart on an ungreased baking sheet. Flatten balls with a fork.

Bake in the preheated oven until edges are set, about 10 minutes. Let cool on the baking sheet for 10 minutes.

Line a tray with waxed paper. Transfer cookies to tray until cooled to room temperature, about 15 minutes, then refrigerate for 30 minutes.

Chewy Chocolate Chip Cookies

Ingredients

1/2 cup butter (softened)

1/2 cup Sukrin Gold

1/3 cup Sukrin Erythritol

1 egg

2 teaspoon vanilla extract

1 cup almond flour

2 tablespoon coconut flour

2 teaspoon baking powder

1/4 teaspoon salt

2/3 cup sugar free chocolate chips

Directions

Cream together softened butter, Sukrin Gold and Sukrin Erythritol with an electric hand mixer until just smooth. Do not over mix.

Add egg and vanilla extract, cream until combined. Add all dry ingredients(almond flour, coconut flour, salt and baking powder). Mix until combined.

With a wooden spoon, fold in chocolate chips.

Spread your cookie dough around the sides of mixing bowl and refrigerate for 30 minutes.

Once your dough is firm, preheat your oven to 375°F and scoop dough on a parchment paper lined baking sheet, 2-3 inches apart.

Bake for about 15 minutes. Cookies will be golden on the edges when done. Let cool after removing from oven.

Nutrition: 73 Calories; 7g Fat; 2g Protein; 1.5g Net Carbohydrates per cookie

Mint Coconut Cookies

Ingredients

2 cups desiccated unsweetened coconut

1/2 cup unsweetened almond milk

1 1/2 tsp peppermint extract

1/2 cup Splenda

3 egg whites

1/4 teaspoon xanthan gum

1 oz 90% or greater cacao dark chocolate

Directions

Combine the coconut, almond milk, peppermint extract, and sweetener in a medium bowl and stir well.

In a separate large bowl whisk the egg whites and xanthan gum together until soft peaks form.

Fold the egg mixture into the coconut mixture until fully combined.

Drop the dough mixture by scoop or tablespoon into 24 mounds onto a parchment-lined cookie sheet. Flatten into disks with your hand or a flat spatula.

Bake in a preheated 325 degree (F) oven for 16 minutes or until slightly firm.

Remove and cool. Place the chocolate in a ziplock bag and melt in the microwave for 30 seconds at a time until just liquid.

Cut a small corner off of the bag and squeeze the chocolate out onto the cookies in a circular pattern. Cool and serve.

Sugar Free Oatmeal Raisin Cookies

Ingredients

1 1/2 cup quick-cooking rolled oats

1/2 cup all-purpose flour

1 teaspoon baking powder

1/2 teaspoon baking soda

1 teaspoon pumpkin pie spice

2 tablespoons Splenda brown sugar

1/3 cup granulated Splenda

2 tablespoons reduced-calorie margarine, melted

1 egg, slightly beaten

1/2 cup unsweetened applesauce

1/4 cup fat-free plain yogurt

1/3 cup raisins

Directions

Preheat oven to 350 degrees. Coat 2 baking sheets with cooking spray.

In a large bowl, combine oats, flour, baking powder, baking soda, pumpkin pie spice, Splenda brown sugar, and granulated Splenda. Add margarine and blend into oats mixture. Add egg, applesauce, yogurt, and raisins. Mix gently to combine.

Drop by tablespoonful to form 24 cookies on prepared baking sheets.

Bake 20 to 22 minutes. Let cool completely on wire racks.

Coconut Vanilla Cookies

Ingredients

1 cup unsalted butter 2 sticks

2 tablespoons water

3/4 cup plus 2 tablespoons Swerve

2 large eggs

1/2 teaspoon pure vanilla extract

1/2 cup Swerve with a touch of blackstrap molasses

1 cup almond flour

1/3 cup coconut flour

1 teaspoon baking soda

1/2 teaspoon baking powder

1/4 teaspoon table salt

4 cups unsweetened flaked coconut

Directions

In medium sized pot, melt butter on medium heat, stirring frequently. Once melted, it should foam, turn a clear golden color, and then become dark brown.

Remove browned butter from heat and pour it and any browned bits into a heat safe measuring cup.

Slowly add enough water to bring measurement back to one cup. Be careful not to pour the cooler water too fast into the hot butter.

Place butter in refrigerator for 1-2 hours or until solid.

Preheat oven to 350°F and line cookie sheets with parchment paper or silicone mat.

Cream white sweetener and browned butter with electric mixture until fluffy.

Add egg and beat until well combined, scraping bowl as needed. Then beat in vanilla.

Mix brown sugar sweetener, almond flour, coconut flour, baking powder, baking soda, and salt in medium bowl.

Pour half of the dry flour mixture into creamed butter mixture and mix until combined. Mix in the other half of the flour mixture. Stir in unsweetened coconut flakes, half at a time.

Scoop dough into 1 tablespoon sized balls on prepared baking sheets, leaving room between to spread. Flatten each dough ball with fingers or spoon.

Bake 10-11 minutes for 1 tablespoon balls. Allow cookies to cool at least 15 minutes before removing to cooling rack

Snickerdoodle Cookies

Ingredients

1 1/2 cups almond flour

1/4 cup butter, salted

1/2 cup pumpkin puree

1 teaspoon vanilla extract

1/2 teaspoon baking powder

1 large egg

1/4 cup erythritol

25 drops Stevia

Topping

1 teaspoon pumpkin pie spice

2 teaspoon Erythritol

Directions

Preheat oven to 350F. Mix all dry ingredients in a bowl.

In a separate bowl, combine the butter, pumpkin puree, vanilla, and liquid stevia and mix.

Mix both bowls together well until a dough is formed. Roll the dough into 15 small balls and set on a cookie sheet.

Press the balls flat and bake for 12-13 minutes.

While the cookies are baking, run 2 tsp erythritol and 1 tsp pumpkin pie spice through a spice grinder.

Once the cookies are done, sprinkle with the topping and let cool completely.

Butter Cookies

Ingredients

1/2 cup butter, softened

1/3 cup granular Splenda

1 teaspoon lemon extract

1 teaspoon vanilla

1 teaspoon lemon zest, from 1 small lemon

1 egg

1 cup almond flour

1/3 cup vanilla whey protein powder

1 teaspoon baking powder

Directions

Put all ingredients in a medium bowl and beat with an electric mixer until creamy for about 1 minute.

Using a 2 teaspoon cookie scoop, scoop 24 balls of the dough onto a silicone or parchment-lined baking sheet. Place them 6 balls across and 4 balls down on the sheet.

Cover the dough balls with a sheet of wax paper. Very gently press them down with the bottom of a glass or small bowl to about 1/4-inch thick.

Carefully remove the wax paper and bake at 350F° for 8-12 minutes or until golden brown. Cool on a wire rack.

Made in the USA
Middletown, DE
20 April 2019